Hedy Lamarr
and Classified Communication

By Virginia Loh-Hagan

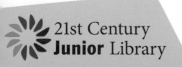
21st Century
Junior Library

Published in the United States of America by
Cherry Lake Publishing
Ann Arbor, Michigan
www.cherrylakepublishing.com

Content Adviser: Kirsten Edwards, MA, Educational Studies
Reading Adviser: Marla Conn MS, Ed., Literacy specialist, Read-Ability, Inc.

Photo Credits: © science photo/Shutterstock.com, Cover, 1; Dishonored Lady film screen shot/Public Domain/Wikimedia Commons, 4; © Monkey Business Images/Shutterstock.com, 6; © tmcphotos/Shutterstock.com, 8; © skeeze/Pixabay.com, 10, 20; © Sura Nualpradid/Shutterstock.com, 12; © Hedy Lamarr (US2292387-1)/United States Patent and Trademark Office/www.uspto.gov, 14; © successo images/Shutterstock.com, 16; © Hayk_Shalunts/Shutterstock.com, 18

Library of Congress Cataloging-in-Publication Data

Names: Loh-Hagan, Virginia, author.
Title: Hedy Lamarr and classified communication / by Virginia Loh-Hagan.
Description: Ann Arbor : Cherry Lake Publishing, [2018] | Series: Women innovators |
    Includes bibliographical references and index. | Audience: Grades 4 to 6.
Identifiers: LCCN 2018003303| ISBN 9781534129122 (hardcover) | ISBN 9781534132320 (pbk.) |
    ISBN 9781534130821 (pdf) | ISBN 9781534134027 (hosted ebook)
Subjects: LCSH: Spread spectrum communications—Juvenile literature. | Lamarr, Hedy, 1913-2000—Juvenile literature. |
    Motion picture actors and actresses—United States—Biography—Juvenile literature.
Classification: LCC TK5102.56.L35 L64 2018 | DDC 621.382—dc23
LC record available at https://lccn.loc.gov/2018003303

Cherry Lake Publishing would like to acknowledge the work of The Partnership for 21st Century Skills.
Please visit *www.p21.org* for more information.

Printed in the United States of America
Corporate Graphics

CONTENTS

Lamarr starred in many movies as a leading lady.

A Woman

How many times a day do you go online? Most of us go online every day. Information is at our fingertips. It's easy to look things up. It's easy to **communicate** with other people. The **Internet** has changed our lives. Thanks to Hedy Lamarr, we can connect to the Internet from almost anywhere.

Lamarr was a famous movie star. But she was also an inventor. She's known as the "mother of **Wi-Fi**."

People type in passwords to use the Internet.

Lamarr was born Hedwig Eva Maria Kiesler. She was born on November 9, 1913, in Vienna, Austria. She later moved to the United States and became a U.S. citizen.

Her mother was a concert pianist. Her father was a banker. Lamarr grew up surrounded by smart, creative people. She was encouraged to think and explore. At 5 years old, she took apart her music

Look!

Look at an old toy you have. Now take it apart, like Lamarr did. Figure out how it works.

Inventors get their ideas from everywhere.

box and then put it back together. She liked to see how things worked.

Lamarr started making movies as a teenager. She first made movies in Europe and then moved to Hollywood. She became a star. Everyone knew her face. She was the model for Snow White, the character in Disney's movie *Snow White and the Seven Dwarfs*. She was called the most beautiful woman in the world.

But she was more than just a pretty face. Lamarr was a wife, mother, and inventor. She was married six times and had three children. She died on January 19, 2000, in Florida.

Lamarr loved learning new things.

An Idea

In 1933, Lamarr married Friedrich
Mandl. He hosted meetings with scientists
and military experts. Lamarr was at his
side. She learned about **innovations** in
the military and in radio. This sparked her
interest in science. But she lost her interest
in Mandl. After four years of marriage, she
left him.

She used what she learned from her
time with Mandl to support the Americans

Music and math are connected. Music can be
described in mathematical terms.

in World War II. She wanted to help fight the **Nazis**.

She worked with George Antheil, a music composer. Together, they created a secret communications system. It was a radio guidance system for **torpedoes**. The guidance system hopped radio **frequencies**. Instead of staying on one frequency channel, it switched and used many channels. This kept information secure so enemies couldn't decode where the torpedoes were going.

Lamarr and Antheil combined what they knew. Lamarr knew about weapons. Antheil knew about player pianos. He wrote

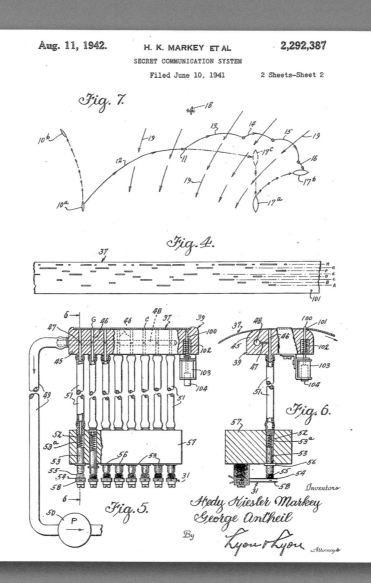

This is a drawing of their patent.

music that required 16 player pianos to match up. This gave them the idea for the frequency hopping. Radio signals hopped different frequencies like notes on a piano. There were 88 frequencies to match 88 piano keys.

Lamarr and Antheil got a **patent** in 1942. They donated it to the U.S. Navy to support the war.

Think!

Think about how music and science are connected. Musicians and scientists are creative problem solvers. Think of other examples combining music and science concepts.

People use Bluetooth technology to play music
on a wireless speaker.

A Legacy

The navy didn't take Lamarr seriously. They couldn't see beyond her good looks. They told her to support the war effort by using her star power to raise money. She did this, but she also helped the future. Her ideas weren't understood until years later.

Lamarr's **legacy** can be seen in today's technology. Her ideas led to Wi-Fi, cell phones, global positioning systems (GPS), Bluetooth, and much more.

Awards recognize people for their work.

Lamarr earned awards for both her acting and her inventing. She has a star on the Hollywood Walk of Fame. She got a Pioneer Award from the Electronic Frontier Foundation. She was the first female to win the Gnass Spirit of Achievement Award. In 2014, Lamarr and Antheil were honored in the National Inventors Hall of Fame.

She invented more than just a communications system. Some of her ideas were big and fancy. For example, she helped design airplanes. But some of her ideas were smaller. For example, she made

Lamarr had a room in her house just for inventing.

pills that fizzed into soda when dropped in water. She never stopped inventing. She said, "Inventions are easy for me to do. I suppose I just came from a different planet."

Make a Guess!

What do you think is the next innovation in computer-based communications? Make a guess.

GLOSSARY

communicate (kuh-MYOO-nih-kate) share or exchange information, news, or ideas

frequencies (FREE-kwuhn-seez) the particular wavebands at which radio stations or other systems broadcast or transmit signals

innovations (in-uh-VAY-shuhnz) new ideas or inventions

Internet (IN-ter-net) the electronic network that allows millions of computers around the world to connect together

legacy (LEG-uh-see) something handed down from one generation to another

Nazi (NAHT-see) a member of the political group that ruled Germany from 1933 to 1945 and was responsible for killing millions of people

patent (PAT-ent) the right from the government to use or sell an invention for a certain number of years

torpedoes (tor-PEE-dohz) underwater bombs shaped like tubes that explode when they hit a target, such as a ship

Wi-Fi (WYE-FYE) the wireless signal that allows computers, smartphones, or other devices to connect to the Internet or communicate with one another

FIND OUT MORE

BOOKS

Gaines, Ann. *Hedy Lamarr*. Vero Beach, FL: Rourke Pub., 2002.

Robbins, Trina. *Hedy Lamarr and a Secret Communication System*. Mankato, MN: Capstone Press, 2007.

Swaby, Rachel. *Trailblazers: 33 Women in Science Who Changed the World*. New York: Delacorte Press, 2016.

WEBSITES

Famous Scientists—Hedy Lamarr
https://www.famousscientists.org/hedy-lamarr/
Learn more about Lamarr's life as a scientist.

Social Studies for Kids—Hedy Lamarr
http://www.socialstudiesforkids.com/articles/worldhistory/hedylamarr.htm
Read about Lamarr's life and invention.

INDEX

ABOUT THE AUTHOR

Dr. Virginia Loh-Hagan is an author, university professor, former classroom teacher, and curriculum designer. She uses Wi-Fi every day. She lives in San Diego with her very tall husband and very naughty dogs. To learn more about her, visit www.virginialoh.com.